500+

Jokes,
Tongue-Twisters,
& Fun Facts

For Kids!

*

J.J. Wiggins

ISBN: 978-1523480432
Edition: 1.2

"There is nothing in the world so irresistibly contagious as laughter and good humor."
— Charles Dickens

Contents

1. People & Things 1

2. Science & Technology 13

3. Around The World 23

4. Plants & Animals 35

5. Food & Entertainment 47

6. Knock-Knock Jokes 57

7. Glossary Of Fun Facts 89

People & Things

Q: Why did the driver pinch his nose?
A: Because his car had gas.

Q: What do you get when you cross a ghost and a tiger?
A: A booger.

Q: Why are ghosts not allowed to scare little children?
A: Because it's taboo.

> **Fun Fact:** If something is 'taboo', it means it's not allowed or unacceptable.

Q: What did the kitten say when the vet gave it a shot?
A: "Me, ow!"

Q: What do you get when you cross a bunny and sticky tape?
A: Hopscotch. (Scotch tape)

Q: What are baby snowmen called?
A: Freezies.

Q: What did the cop say to the bad farmer?
A: "Your goose is cooked!"

> **Fun Fact:** If somebody tells you: 'your goose is cooked', it means you are in big trouble!

Q: What game are little clocks good at?
A: Tick tock toe.

Q: Why was one clock ticked off at the other?
A: Because it tocked too much. (talked)

Q: Where do liars learn to lie?
A: At the lie-brary.

Q: Why did Mary scream when she entered the library?
A: She saw a bunch of bookworms!

> **Fun Fact:** A 'bookworm' is someone who enjoys reading or studying.

Q: Why was the car tire embarrassed?
A: Because it was flat-ulent.

Q: What did the doctor tell the old gingerbread man?
A: "You'll need to use a candy cane."

Q: Why was the janitor so surprised when he saw the litter on the floor?
A: Because the puppies barked at him!

> **Fun Fact:** A group of puppies or kittens is called a 'litter.'

Q: Why didn't the zookeeper hire the bear from Australia?
A: Because it wasn't koala-fied for the job! (qualified)

Q: Why were all the king's men so short?
A: Because they were his foot soldiers.

Q: Why did the little boy sit on the mushroom?
A: Because his mom told him it was a toadstool.

Q: What did the farmer say to the lazy vegetable?
A: "Stop being a couch potato!"

Q: What do you call money made out of clay?
A: Play-dough.

> Fun Fact: 'Dough' is a slang word that means 'money.'

Q: What do you call one foot that follows the other everywhere?
A: Its sidekick.

> Fun Fact: A 'sidekick' is a close friend or companion who follows you everywhere on adventures.

Q: Why did the umbrella turn down the sun's dinner invitation?
A: Because it wanted to take a rain check.

> Fun Fact: 'To take a rain check' means you have an appointment with someone but you can't make it, so you want to change it to another day.

Q: What do you call a thirteen year old kid who complains a lot?
A: A tee-nagger.

Q: What do you call it when a bunch of apes buy and sell things?
A: Monkey business.

Q: What do you call poop that's not real?
A: Sham-poo!

Q: Where do monsters park their cars?
A: In the grrrr-age.

Q: What hairstyle do zombies get at the salon?
A: Dreadlocks.

Q: What do you call someone who dives into a toilet?
A: A plunger.

Q: Why did the mouth feel really stupid after going to the dentist?
A: It had its wisdom teeth removed.

> <u>Fun Fact:</u> Did you know... you don't start growing your wisdom teeth until you're twenty years old!

Q: What did the man say when his gun ran out of bullets?
A: "Shoot!"

Q: Why did James fail the driving exam?
A: He couldn't read sign language.

> **Fun Fact:** Sign Language is a way to talk to other people by using your hands. It's used for communicating with deaf people.

Q: Why didn't the circle understand the joke?
A: Because it couldn't get it straight.

Q: What kind of guns do police bees use?
A: Bee-bee guns.

Q: What are letters afraid of most?
A: Stamp-edes! (stampede)

Q: Why do lines always do better than circles in races?
A: Because they get straight to the point.

Q: Why was the hole mad at the grave digger?
A: Because it was bored to death.

Q: What did the new sock say to the old, worn-out sock?
A: "It socks to be you!"

Q: What did the farmer's wife tell him to do when he couldn't fall asleep?
A: "Try counting sheep."

Q: Where do shoes go to become stronger?
A: To boot-camp.

Q: What do skeletons drive in the winter?
A: A zam-bone-i! (zamboni)

> Fun Fact: A 'zamboni' is a vehicle used to clean and smooth the surface of ice, for example the ice in a skating rink. It was developed in 1949 by a man named Frank Zamboni.

Q: What do telephones like to read?
A: Phone books.

Q: What do you get when you cross a ghost with a former US president?
A: George Boo-sh. (George Bush)

Q: What is found between June and December?
A: JASON.

> **Fun Fact:** If you take the first letters of 'July, August, September, October, November', you get 'JASON!'

Q: What would Valentine's Day be called if it happened in October?
A: Fall-entine's Day.

Q: Why didn't Jimmy feel like playing with his skateboard?
A: Because he was skate-bored.

Q: How did the ballerina cross the road?
A: By pirouetting every step of the way!

Q: What did the nose say to the mouth after dinner?
A: "Smells like garlic!"

Q: Why couldn't the cat lady speak?
A: Because the cat's got her tongue.

> Fun Fact: 'Cat's got your tongue' just means somebody wants to say something but doesn't know what to say because they can't think.

Q: Why can't funny people ever be serious?
A: Because they're always clowning around!

Q: Why didn't the clown get the job?
A: Because he forgot to put a smile on his face for the interview.

Q: How can you tell when a toilet is embarrassed?
A: When it is flushed.

> Fun Fact: Someone who's 'flushed' has a very red face because they feel embarrassed.

Q: What did the tooth say after its appointment with the dentist?
A: "Thanks, it's very filling!"

> **Fun Fact:** You go to the dentist for a filling when your teeth have cavities. Don't forget to brush your teeth!

Q: What sound does a fly make?
A: "Zzzip!"

FUNNY SOUNDS

It's time for some silliness. Say the lines below 5 times really fast without laughing!

Blue poop hoop loop.

Beep pop leap hop bleep.

Jiggle giggle igloo pig glue wiggle.

Wow whoa ow owe pow.

Lock lick clock luck cluck lock click.

Swish swash wash lush slush wish.

Pong bong belong gong long.

Lung among a monk a punk gunk.

Happy puppy poppy hippy yippee.

Dad a dumb dam a doom dim.

Now, get a friend or family member to give it a try!

12   PEOPLE & THINGS

Science & Technology

Q: Where can spiders go to order food?
A: On the web!

> **Fun Fact:** The 'Web' is another word for the Internet. It's called a 'Web' because people from all over the world are connected to each other.

Q: How do one-eyed monsters do research for their homework?
A: They use an En-cyclop-edia.

> **Fun Fact:** A 'cyclops' is a giant with one humongous eye in the middle of its forehead!

Q: Where do witches get recipes for their potions?
A: On Wicca-pedia.

Q: How do leprechauns and rainbows talk to one another?
A: With Sky-pe.

Q: How do eyeballs talk to each other?
A: With iPhones!

> **Fun Fact:** Did you know... that company that make iPhones is called 'Apple.'

Q: What do you call fake smart phones?
A: iPhonies.

Q: What do you call a photo album with lots of selfies?
A: A face book.

> **Fun Fact:** Did you know... the founder of Facebook is Mark Zuckerberg and his last name, 'Zuckerberg', means 'sugar mountain' in German! How funny is that?
>
> What does *your* name mean?

Q: How did the slime find its way home?
A: It got directions from Goo-gle!

> **Fun Fact:** The popular search engine, Google, got its name from the word, googol, which means a number starting with 1, followed by a hundred zeros!

Q: How do birds talk to each other on the Internet?
A: They tweet!

Q: What do you call one Lego piece on the street?
A: Roadblock.

Q: What do you call millions of Lego pieces on the street?
A: Roblox.

Q: What game do geniuses play after school?
A: Mind-craft. (Minecraft)

Q: What do you call a game console falling from a 100-story tall building?
A: Nintendo Weeeeee!

Q: What do you call an ant that plays with chemicals?
A: Sci-ant-ist! (scientist)

Q: How do turtles see into space?
A: They use a shell-escope! (telescope)

Q: Why did the alien cross the road?
A: To return to its spaceship before anybody spots it, of course!

Q: What do call a very flexible robot?
A: An acro-bot. (acrobat)

Q: What do you call a robot ant?
A: An ant-droid. (android)

> **Fun Fact:** An 'android' is a machine that looks and behaves like a human.

Q: What street do cows live on?
A: Milky Way.

> **Fun Fact:** Did you know... our Earth and sun are found in a galaxy called the Milky Way. The Milky Way has about 200-400 billion stars!

Q: Where do alien ants come from?
A: Ant-dromeda. (Andromeda)

> **Fun Fact:** Andromeda is the closest galaxy to the Milky Way at about 2.2 million light years away!

Q: What do you call a robot that's good at repairing things?
A: A mech-anic.

Q: Why is the ocean blue?
A: Because it's under the weather.

Q: Why was the ocean mad at the beach?
A: Because it wouldn't wave back!

Q: How does the ground say hi to the clouds?
A: "What's up?"

Q: What do you call a bunch of elephants dancing?
A: Earthquake!

Q: Why was the snowman afraid of the avalanche?
A: Because it was actually a lava-lanche!

> <u>**Fun Fact:**</u> Did you know...'lava' is rock that's turned into liquid, and it's very, very hot!

Q: What do you call a very, very, very, very small sheep?
A: An amoebaaaa. (amoeba)

Q: What do call a very, very, very, very, small dog?
A: A fido-plankton. (phytoplankton)

> **Fun Fact:** Amoeba and phytoplankton are very, very small living things that you can only see with a microscope. They live in wet places!

Q: What sickness do horses get when they eat too much?
A: Hay fever.

> **Fun Fact:** Having 'hay fever' means things like dust and pollen make you sneeze and your eyes itchy and watery!

Q: What game do lights play at recess?
A: Laser tag!

> **Fun Fact:** Laser tag is something you can actually do in real life! Have you tried it?

Q: Why was the computer yawning?
A: Because it was key-bored.

Q: What do call a spider that likes to take pictures?
A: A shutterbug.

Q: Why couldn't the horses understand the cows?
A: The cows were using Moo-rse Code. (Morse code)

> **Fun Fact:** Morse code is a way to send secret messages to other people using clicking sounds or light.

Q: What didn't the computer and the mouse like each other?
A: Because they didn't click.

> **Fun Fact:** 'To not click with someone' means you don't get along with this person.

Q: What can you ride that's lighter than a feather?
A: An air-plane.

Q: What do you call a pterodactyl in the sky?
A: A dino-soar!

Q: What do you call a pie flying through the air at 600 mph?
A: A pie-lot. (pilot)

> **Fun Fact:** Did you know... the record for the fastest flight speed is over 2000 mph, more than 3 times the speed of sound!

Q: Why didn't the moon want any more food?
A: Because it was already full.

> **Fun Fact:** Did you know... a full moon occurs once about every 27 days.

SILLY PHRASES

It's time for some more silliness! Again, say these lines 5 times and try not to laugh!

Poor Pete pooped purple popcorn.

Sally saw seven silly snakes skipping school.

Willy washes wieners Wednesdays.

Haunted houses hate hairy horses.

She sees sleepy sheep sweeping steamy ships.

Cats can't count 'cause counting causes chaos.

Lisa licked leftover lamb.

Zippy zebras zoomed.

My mom made me mega muffins.

Dogs do dirty dandruff dance.

Fun Fact: You can actually make your own purple popcorn! Just add purple food coloring before you microwave the popcorn kernels.

Do you know somebody named Pete or Willy? If so, get them to read these silly phrases!

Around The World

Q: What do insects use to find accommodations when they travel?
A: AirBee-n-Bee!

Q: What do you call a snowman that travels a lot?
A: A snow-globetrotter.

Q: Where do beavers go for vacation?
A: To Amster-dam!

> **Fun Fact:** Did you know... Amsterdam is in the Netherlands, a country in Europe.

Q: Why couldn't Sam understand the toasts?
A: Because they were French.

Q: How do French people say 'I love you' when they're in England?
A: "Je Thames!"

> **Fun Fact:** The correct way to say 'I love you' in French is 'Je t'aime.'

Q: What do call a very famous painting of a cow?
A: The Moo-na Lisa. (Mona Lisa)

> **Fun Fact:** The Mona Lisa is a very famous painting which can be seen in the Louvre, a museum in France. It was painted by an artist named Leonardo da Vinci.

Q: What do you get when you cross a hummingbird and cheese?
A: A coli-Brie. (colibri)

> **Fun Fact:** Colibri is another word for hummingbird, and Brie is a type of cheese!

Q: How is an apple's skin so red?
A: It puts on rouge.

Q: Where do snails go to rent a car?
A: To Es-car-got. (escargot)

> **Fun Fact:** 'Escargot' is a French word meaning 'snail.'

Q: What do you call a Roman alligator holding a sword?
A: gladi-gator! (gladiator)

Q: What do pigs learn in Language Studies?
A: Pig Latin.

> **Fun Fact:** Did you know… Pig Latin is a made-up language that you can use to talk to other people in secret. It's English with a twist!

> **How it works:**
> 1. For words beginning with consonants, move those letters to the end of the word and add '-ay.'

> 'hello' becomes 'ello-ay'
> 'plan' becomes 'an-play'

> 2. For words beginning with vowels, just add '-yay' to the end of the word.

> 'it' becomes 'it-yay'
> 'animal' becomes 'animal-yay'

> **Examples:**
> Bedroom = Ed-bay oom-ray.
> How are you? = Ow-hay are-yay ou-yay?
> What's up? = At's-whay up-yay?

> With these two simple rules, you can start speaking to people in code. Of course, they have to know Pig Latin, too. So go teach your friends!

Q: What language does a German Shepherd speak?
A: Dogs can't talk, silly!

Q: What did the German shepherd say when he saw his friend?
A: "Guten Tag!"

> Fun Fact: 'Guten Tag' is German and it means 'Hello' or 'Good day.'

Q: What do you call the baddest sausage in the pack?
A: The Wurst.

> Fun Fact: 'Wurst' is also German, and it means 'sausage.'

Q: Where do cooties come from?
A: Germ-any!

Q: What is a slime's favorite type of drink?
A: Ouzo.

Q: What did the sheep have for dinner?
A: Baa-baa ganoush. (baba ganoush)

Q: What did the sheep have for dessert?
A: Baa-klava. (baklava)

> Fun Fact: Baklava is a pastry from the Middle East filled with nuts and honey. Yummy!

Q: Where are electric pokémon found?
A: On Machu Picchu.

> Fun Fact: Did you know...Machu Picchu is a real place you can visit. It's found high up in the mountains in South America and belonged to the Inca, a civilization that ruled it over 500 years ago!

Q: What do tourist cats do when they're in Egypt?
A: They visit the Purr-amids. (the Pyramids)

> Fun Fact: There's a giant statue by the pyramids called a 'sphinx', which is a creature that's half-human, half-lion!

Q: Where do pigs go to relax on the beach?
A: To Porkto Rico. (Puerto Rico)

Q: Where do cute little birds come from?
A: The Canary Islands.

Q: Where do beetles get their cars?
A: From Mada-gas-car!

Q: What do wild pigs like to eat when they're in the Ukraine?
A: Boar-scht. (Borscht)

> **Fun Fact:** 'Borscht' is a kind of soup from the Ukraine. Its main ingredient is beet, a vegetable that turns pretty much everything red!

Q: Where should people who can't stop eating food go live?
A: In Hungary. (hungry)

Q: Which country probably doesn't like visitors very much?
A: No-way. (Norway)

Q: Where are cooking oil made?
A: In grease. (Greece)

Q: What do moose use to style their hair?
A: Mousse.

Q: Where do king and queen pigs live?
A: In Bucking-ham Palace.

> Fun Fact: Buckingham Palace is found in England, and it's where queens used to live! Today, it's used for special events hosted by the royal family.

Q: Where do deer come from?
A: Tim-buck-tu! (Timbuktu)

> Fun Fact: Timbuktu is a city in Mali, a country in Africa.

Q: Where do wild pigs come from?
A: The Ham-azon Rainforest. (the Amazon Rainforest)

Q: Where do cows go when they die?
A: To Moo-topia. (utopia)

> Fun Fact: Did you know... 'utopia' is a place where everything is perfect. Complete peace and no wars.

Q: Where do sheep go for vacation?
A: To the Baa-hamas. (the Bahamas)

Q: Which US states always ask a lot questions?
A: Why-oming and Al-ask-a.

Q: Where do clowns go for vacation?
A: To Hahaha-waii. (Hawaii)

Q: Where do owls go for vacation?
A: To Honohoohoo, Hawaii. (Honolulu)

Q: Where do vampire trains live?
A: In Train-sylvania. (Transylvania)

> **Fun Fact:** Did you know... Transylvania is a region in Romania, a country in Europe. It's often seen as a place of magic and mystery, and many vampire movies use it as a setting.

Q: Which holiday do kitchens in Mexico celebrate?
A: Sinko de Mayo. (Cinco de Mayo)

Q: Who do horses learn to play soccer from?
A: Neigh-mar. (Neymar)

> **Fun Fact:** Neymar da Silva Santos Júnior is a Brazilian soccer player who has won a lot of awards. He is considered one of the best soccer players in the world.

Q: What do leeches like to eat?
A: Lychee.

> **Fun Fact:** Lychee is a white, juicy fruit from Asia.

Q: What kind of car do Jedis drive?
A: A To-yoda (Toyota)

Q: What kind of car do bears drive?
A: A Furrr-ari. (Ferrari)

Q: What kind of car do pigs drive?
A: A Porsche.

Q: What kind of car do sheep drive?
A: A Lamb-orghini.

MORE SILLY PHRASES

There's a chicken in the kitchen and its chin is itchin.'

Wait a while, while I wave to Willy's whale.

The book crook took the hook from the cook.

Pikachu chews cashews on Machu Picchu.

Critters give me jitters, and so do baby sitters.

Mom is stuffin' the muffin in the oven.

Monica got a harmonica for Hanukkah.

I met the vet who gave my pet a jet.

Who knew Sue knew kung-fu? You.

Gnats gnaw at naked gnomes at night.

Fun Fact: All over the world, Jewish people celebrate Hanukkah instead of Christmas.

34   AROUND THE WORLD

Plants & Animals

Q: What's the smelliest dog in the world?
A: A poodle.

Q: What do you call a dog with a sombrero?
A: El Poocho.

Q: What do you get when you cross a blimp with a sheep?
A: A bleep.

Q: Why didn't the owl do its homework?
A: Because it didn't give a hoot.

> **Fun Fact:** 'To not give a hoot' means you don't care about something.

Q: What do you get when you glue two cats together?
A: An octo-puss.

Q: What do you call two flowers that are best of friends?
A: Rose-buds.

Q: What do you call a kangaroo that works at a hotel?
A: A bellhop.

> **Fun Fact:** A bellhop is someone who works at a hotel and helps carry people's bags to their rooms.

Q: Why was the mother gorilla mad at her children?
A: Because they were monkey-ing around!

Q: How did the dog get lost in the forest?
A: It was barking up the wrong tree.

> **Fun Fact:** If you say 'you're barking up the wrong tree' to somebody, it means you think they misunderstood something or you want to tell them they are totally wrong!

> Have you heard this expression before? Try to use it with your friends and family!

Q: What do you call two vegetables that are very good friends?
A: Bro-ccolis.

Q: What is a dog's favorite vegetable?
A: Collie-flower.

Q: What kind of vegetable belongs in the zoo?
A: A zoo-cchini. (zucchini)

Q: What is a spider's favorite vegetable?
A: Spin-ach.

Q: What did the strawberry do for work before it retired?
A: It was a li-berry-an! (librarian)

Q: Where do pigs put their savings?
A: In a piggy bank.

Q: How do skunks say goodbye to one another?
A: "I'll smell you later."

Q: Why are bees the least favorite guests at a party?
A: Because they are buzzkills.

> **Fun Fact:** A 'buzzkill' is someone or something that stops people from enjoying themselves.

Q: What did the mother hare call her son?
A: "Bunnykins!"

Q: What did the mother bee tell her son before he went out the beehive?
A: "Beeee careful out there!"

Q: How do camels hide from dangers in the desert?
A: By using camel-flage. (camouflage)

Q: What happened when the snake couldn't get its food?
A: It threw a hissy fit.

Q: What's common between fish and music?
A: They both have scales.

Q: Why wasn't the turkey at Thanksgiving dinner?
A: Because it was already stuffed.

> Fun Fact: People from Canada celebrate Thanksgiving in October, while people from the United States celebrate it in November!
>
> When do *you* celebrate Thanksgiving?

Q: How did one sheep say goodbye to the other?
A: "I'll see ewe later!"

> Fun Fact: An 'ewe' is a female sheep.

Q: What is the most beautiful insect in the world?
A: The ladybug.

Q: Which insect only appears during one month of the year?
A: The June bug.

Q: What do you call mean fish that spread germs?
A: Barra-cooties. (barracuda)

Q: What is a fish's favorite motto?
A: Carpe Diem.

> **Fun Fact:** 'Carpe Diem' is Latin, and it means 'seize the day.' It's an expression meaning to enjoy the present and not worry about the future.

Q: What sounds does a horse make when it's pretending to be a dog?
A: "Hoof hoof. Grrr!!!"

Q: What do you call a group of really bad cows?
A: The moo-fia. (Mafia)

Q: Where do animals go to get advice on money?
A: To an ac-cow-ntant. (accountant)

Q: What's a vegetable that's found in the ocean?
A: A sea cucumber.

Q: Where do sheep go for higher education?
A: To ewe-niversity. (university)

Q: What do you call a snake that's not good at math?
A: Anything but an adder!

Q: What do you call a butterfly that can't fly?
A: Butter.

Q: What do you get when you cross a pig and a whale?
A: A porca.

> **Fun Fact:** Did you know... 'orca' is another name for killer whale.

Q: What do you get when you cross an elephant and a ghost?
A: An elephantom!

Q: What do you call an annoying unicorn that buzzes?
A: Horsefly.

Q: What do you call fish that don't belong to you?
A: Angel fish! (ain't your fish)

Q: What do vegetables get if they don't brush their roots everyday?
A: Ginger-vitis.

> **Fun Fact:** You can get gingivitis if you don't brush your teeth everyday. It makes your gums red and your breath smell!

Q: Why wasn't the little bird allowed to fly to its friend's nest?
A: Because it was grounded.

Q: What do bees do after they get married?
A: Go on a honeymoon.

Q: Why do bees' hairs smell so sweet?
A: Because they use a honeycomb.

Q: What can you find at a store run by insects?
A: Flea bargains.

Q: What kind of flower is the easiest to remember?
A: The forget-me-not.

Q: Why did the chicken dash across the road?
A: Because it was actually a roadrunner.

> **Fun Fact:** A 'roadrunner' is a small, brown and white bird that lives in the desert and can run very, very fast.

Q: What do vampire bees like to drink after dinner?
A: Neck-tar. (nectar)

> **Fun Fact:** Nectar is a sweet, sugary liquid that plants produce to attract insects such as bees.

Q: What kind of dog likes going to church?
A: A Saint Bernard.

> **Fun Fact:** Saint Bernards are the biggest breed of dog in the world!

Q: How do cool pigs greet one another?
A: With a secret ham-shake!

Q: What do you call a happy chipmunk?
A: Chipper.

Q: Why was the bird scared of the worm?
A: Because it was a chicken.

Q: What happened to the egg that had to do a speech in front of lots of people?
A: It cracked under pressure.

Q: What do you call a dog that's really good at football?
A: A Golden Receiver.

Q: Where do mother pigs leave their piglets?
A: In the playpen.

Q: Why is it useless to argue with a cow?
A: Because it's a moo-t point. (moot point)

Q: Where do fish put their money?
A: In the river bank.

Q: What do you call a goldfish with no money?
A: A fish.

Q: Why was the squirrel afraid of the tree?
A: Because there were too many nuts hanging around.

Q: Why don't crabs make good friends?
A: Because they're shellfish! (selfish)

> Fun Fact: 'Shellfish' are a type of aquatic animal that has a shell, such as oysters, lobsters, and crabs.

Q: Why did the mouse break up with her boyfriend?
A: Because he was too cheesy for her.

Q: What do you call a kangaroo that can't hop?
A: A kan't-garoo!

Q: Where do farm animals go when they're not feeling well?
A: To the duck-tor's!

Q: What can you find in a church for insects?
A: Bee-lievers!

TONGUE-TWISTERS

Here's another challenge for you. Try not to get your tongue twisted!

Peas please police for peace.

Cats can't catch rats 'cause they're chitchattin.'

The walrus caught a very wacky virus.

We read very weird stories every week.

Which wristwatch does Rich want?

Chris misses Christmas 'cause Chris's missus is cross.

Sugar boogers sure are good for beggars.

Big piglets have big pig legs.

Mr. Fisher fishes fresh jellyfishes.

Bulls wow cows at cattle pow-wows.

Food & Entertainment

Q: What is SpongeBob's sister's name?
A: SpongeBarb SquarePants.

Q: What do viruses like to watch at the movie theater?
A: "Star Warts."

Q: What movie do silly dwarfs like to watch?
A: "Snow White and the Seven Doofuses."

Q: What is a snowman's favorite animated film?
A: "Frozen."

Q: What movie do cows like to watch?
A: "Ho-moooo Alone."

Q: What do you call a cooking show about fish?
A: "Frying Nemo."

Q: What TV show do sloths like to watch?
A: "American Idle."

Q: Why did the pig join the singing competition?
A: Because it had good chops.

Q: What do you call a baby girl who can sing really well?
A: Lady Gaa Gaa.

Q: Where do stones and pebbles go to enjoy music?
A: To a rock concert.

Q: What is a rock's favorite band to listen to?
A: The Rolling Stones.

Q: What is a sheep's favorite rock band?
A: Ewe-2. (U2)

> **Fun Fact:** U2 is an Irish rock band that's still very popular today.

Q: What do you call a few car tires in the garage jamming on their instruments?
A: A rubber band.

Q: Which musical instrument are skeletons good at?
A: The trom-bone.

Q: What do you call a concert made up of people who can't play instruments?
A: A sym-phony.

Q: What do ghosts do when they don't like a performance?
A: They boo and disappear.

Q: Why can't cats ever finish watching a movie?
A: Because they keep paws-ing it!

Q: How did the fish escape from Oz?
A: By clicking its flippers.

Q: What kind of horse can you not ride?
A: A pommel horse.

Q: Which Olympic sport are numbers good at?
A: Figure skating.

Q: What is the most useless kind of exercise to do if you want to lose weight?
A: Diddly squats.

Q: What exercises are bananas good at?
A: Splits.

Q: Why didn't the rabbit want to go out and play?
A: Because it was having a bad hare day.

Q: What kind of bee can you throw around in the park?
A: A frisbee!

Q: What do girl bees wear to the beach?
A: Bee-kinis!

Q: Where do cockroaches go surfing?
A: In the micro-wave!

Q: Why didn't the elephants want to go swimming?
A: Because they forgot their trunks!

Q: Why couldn't the pig finish the marathon?
A: Because it tore its ham-string.

> **Fun Fact:** Your hamstring is the soft part found behind your knees!

Q: Why did the crowd boo the chicken at the baseball game?
A: Because it committed a fowl.

Q: What do piglets like to do at the amusement park?
A: Go on piggyback rides!

Q: What do spoons and forks play when no one's watching?
A: Bowl-ing.

Q: Why couldn't the bread get home?
A: It was stuck in a peanut butter and traffic jam.

Q: Where do deer go for coffee?
A: To Star-bucks!

> **Fun Fact:** Did you know... there are over 20,000 Starbucks coffee shops in the world!

Q: What do pigs eat for breakfast?
A: Peanut udder and Ham.

Q: How did one dog ask the other if it wanted to go for lunch?
A: "Do you want to grab a bite with me?"

Q: When did the chicken cross the road?
A: Before it was cooked.

Q: What happened to the pig that sat in the sun for too long?
A: It became pork roast.

Q: Where do numbers go to buy snacks?
A: To the 7-Eleven.

Q: What do you call a poodle tanning on the beach?
A: A hot dog!

Q: What do you get when you mix an assassin with dough and put them in the oven for 45 minutes?
A: A ninja-bread man.

Q: Why was the mouse sad after breakfast?
A: Because it had blue cheese.

> **Fun Fact:** Blue cheese is a very strong type of cheese containing blue mold. It has a very strong smell that most people can't handle!

Q: What did the squirrel say when he couldn't find his food?
A: "Ah, nuts!"

Q: What do kittens always say when asking for food?
A: "Pawweease!"

Q: What is Dracula's favorite drink?
A: Bloody Mary.

Q: What subject do sodas enjoy most?
A: Fizz-ed. (Phys-Ed)

Q: What is a kangaroo's favorite drink?
A: Hopscotch.

Q: What is the coldest fruit in the world?
A: The winter melon.

Q: What kind of cookies do plants like?
A: Gingersnaps.

Q: What is a relative of the paper towel?
A: The nap-kin.

> **Fun Fact:** The word 'kin' refers to all the people in your family.

Q: What do sheep like to eat at the amusement park?
A: Cotton candy.

Q: What is the simplest way to cook an egg?
A: Over easy.

Q: What is a skunk's favorite snack?
A: Mar-shmell-ows. (marshmallows)

Q: Where do dogs go to get treats?
A: To the bark-ery. (bakery)

Q: What do you get when you put a bunch of bugs in a blender?
A: Beetle juice.

Q: What job did the plate get at the restaurant?
A: It was a dish washer.

Q: What do kitchen bowls do when they're filled with food?
A: Have a bowl-movement. (bowel movement)

TRICKY WORDS

Here are some tricky words. See if you can say them correctly!

Bow, row, sow, now, low, how, tow, cow.

Bear, tear, hear, dear, wear, near.

Nation, mansion, cushion, ocean, Martian.

Cut, but, put, gut, strut.

Tint, mint, hint, lint, pint.

Root, boot, loot, foot, soot.

Mean, clean, bean, Sean, lean.

Weight, eight, freight, height.

Dough, cough, tough, through, bough.

Precious, delicious, gracious, malicious.

Knock-Knock Jokes

Knock knock.
   Who's there?
Tobias.
   Tobias who?
Aren't you going Tobias some ice cream?

Knock knock.
   Who's there?
Boo.
   Boo who?
Aw, don't cry!

Knock knock.
   Who's there?
Your friend.
   Your friend who?
Did you already forget my name?

Knock knock.
   Who's there?
China.
   China who?
Are you China be funny?

Knock knock.
Who's there?
Dee.
Dee who?
Put some deodorant on! You're stinkin' up the place.

Knock knock.
Who's there?
Beach.
Beach who?
I'm gonna Beach you up if you don't give me your lunch!

Knock knock.
Who's there?
Pasta.
Pasta who?
Could you Pasta salt, please?

Knock knock.
Who's there?
Justin.
Justin who?
You're Justin time to see my new pet turkey!

Knock knock.
Who's there?
Ken.
Ken who?
Ken you open the door already? It's freezing out here!

Knock knock.
Who's there?
Thomas.
Thomas who?
You're going Thomas the school bus if you don't come out soon!

Knock knock.
Who's there?
Wanda.
Wanda who?
What do you Wanda do today?

Knock knock.
Who's there?
Jack.
Jack who?
Jacuzzi!

Knock knock.
Who's there?
Mike
Mike who?
Pass me the Mike 'cause it's my turn to sing!

Knock knock.
Who's there?
Woo.
Woo who?
Why are you so happy?

Knock knock.
Who's there?
Garbage.
Garbage who?
It's your Garbage, you know, from the kitchen. I'm starting to smell so take me out!

Knock knock.
Who's there?
Maurice.
Maurice who?
Would you like some Mau-rice?

Knock knock.
Who's there?
Mimi.
Mimi who?
Me, me! It's me. Now open the door!

Knock knock.
Who's there?
Wade.
Wade who?
Wade a minute, I'm at the wrong house!

Knock knock.
Who's there?
Duck.
Duck wh-ow!?
I told you to duck!

Knock knock.
Who's there?
Pia.
Pia who?
Pee-ew! It smells.

Knock knock.
Who's there?
Lion.
Lion who?
Quit Lion around and come out and play!

Knock knock.
Who's there?
Doorbell repairman.
Finally! Can you fix it?

Knock knock.
Who's there?
Billy Butterfingers.
Billy Butterfingers who?
Do you know somebody else named Billy Butterfingers?

Moo moo.
Who's there?
Moo.
Moo who?
Mooooo!
Johnny, it's that cow from the farm again. Just ignore it.

Knock knock.
　　Who's there?
Eden.
　　Eden who?
I'm Eden a hamburger!

Ding dong.
　　It works!

Knock knock.
　　Who's there?
Ivana.
　　Ivana who?
Ivana come in, so open the door!

Knock knock.
　　Who's there?
Ashley.
　　Ashley who?
Are you Ashley gonna open the door?

Knock knock.
　　Who's there?
Joanna.
　　Joanna who?
Joanna go to the movies with me?

Knock knock.
Who's there?
Little old lady.
Little old lady who?
I didn't know you could yodel!

Knock knock.
Who's there?
William.
William who?
I just told you. I am Will.

Knock knock.
Who's there?
Delong.
Delong who?
I've got Delong house number.

Knock knock.
Who's there?
Sorry, wrong door!

Knock knock.
Who's there?
You.
You who?
Aw, stop flirting with me!

Knock knock.
Who's there?
Police.
Police who?
Police let me in.

Knock knock.
Who's there?
Towel.
Towel who?
I'll Towel you, but let me in first!

Knock knock.
Just a minute!

Knock knock.
Who's there?
Lettuce.
Lettuce who?
Lettuce in right now!

Knock knock.
Who's there?
Gopher.
Gopher who?
Do you wanna Gopher a drink with me?

Knock knock.
  Who's there?
Anju.
  Anju who?
Anju gonna open the door for me?

Knock knock.
  Who's there?
Hannah.
  Hannah who?
Are you just gonna Hannah round while I wait outside?

Knock knock.
  Who's there?
Mommy.
  Mommy who?
Sweetie, can you open the door? Mommy forgot her keys.

Knock knock.
  Who's there?
Pikachu.
  Pikachu who?
I'm here to Pikachu up!

Knock knock.
　　Who's there?
Howie.
　　Howie who?
Do you know Howie are getting to the zoo?

Knock knock.
　　Come in!

Knock knock.
　　Who's there?
Gemini.
　　Gemini who?
Jim and I are going to the park. Wanna join us?

Knock knock.
　　Who's there?
Stella.
　　Stella who?
Is there Stella school today?

Knock knock.
　　I'm coming out!

Knock knock.
　Who's there?
Luke.
　Luke who?
I'm Luke in for my friend.

Knock knock.
　Who's there?
Billy.
　Billy who?
Mom! Grandma forgot my name again. I thinks she's going crazy.

Knock knock.
　Who's there?
...
　Who's th-!?
Surprise!!!

Knock knock.
　Who's there?
Why.
　Why who?
Why do you want to know my name?

Knock knock.
Go away or I'm calling the police!

Knock knock.
Who's there?
Darren.
Darren who?
Is Darren elephant in your house?

Knock knock.
Who's there?
Kenya.
Kenya who?
Kenya stop asking that! Just open the door.

Knock knock.
Who's there?
Dara.
Dara who?
Is Dara good knock-knock joke in this book?

Knock knock.
Who's ther-?
Nevermind, I found the keys!

Knock knock.
Who's there?
Ketchup.
Ketchup who?
**We haven't seen each other in ages.
Let's Ketchup!**

**Knock knock,
knock knock knock,
knock.**
Who's there?
Oh, did I get the secret knock wrong?

Knock knock.
Who's there?
Nascar.
Nascar who?
**I have a Nascar in my garage, do you
wanna see it?**

Knock knock.
Who's there?
Topher.
Topher who?
**Just to let you know, there's a Topher
one deal today at Walmart. Bye!**

Knock knock.
   Who's there?
Alaska.
   Alaska who?
Can Alaska question?

Knock knock.
   Who's there?
Iowa.
   Iowa who?
Iowa lot of money to the bank!

Knock knock.
   Who's there?
Mary.
   Mary who?
Me. Will you Mary me?

Knock knock.
   Who's there?
Adeel.
   Adeel who?
Boy have I got Adeel for you!

Knock knock.
    Who's there?
Letter.
    Letter who?
Are you gonna Letter dog out to play?

Knock knock.
    Who's there?
Warren.
    Warren who?
I'm hear to Warren you about the storm!

Knock knock.
    Who's there?
Colin.
    Colin who?
I'm Colin the police if you don't let me in.

Knock knock.
    Who's there?
Baba.
    Baba who?
Baa baa, black sheep, have you any wool?

Knock knock.
> Who's there?

FBI.
> FBI wh-?

Open the door now or we're breaking it down!

> Fun Fact: The FBI is the United States' intelligence and security service. It stands for 'Federal Bureau of Investigation.'

Knock knock.
> Who's there?

Suri.
> Suri who?

I'm Suri about the mess I made.

Knock knock.
> Who's there?

Josh.
> Josh who?

I Josh want you to open the door.

Knock knock.
> Who's there?

Yule.
> Yule who?

Come out and Yule see!

Knock knock.
   Who's there?
Eva.
   Eva who?
Have you Eva wondered who invented knock-knock jokes?

> **Fun Fact:** Knock-knock jokes are believed to be first used in one of Shakespeare's plays, but nobody really knows who invented them!

Knock knock.
   Who's there?
June.
   June who?
Did June know that I've been waiting out here for ages!

Knock knock.
   Who's there?
Barry.
   Barry who?
Do you wanna go to the li-Barry with me?

Knock knock.
Who's there?
Cal.
Cal who?
Supercalifragilisticexpialidocious.

Fun Fact: Did you know... the word 'supercalifragilisticexpialidocious' doesn't actually mean anything!

Knock knock.
Who's there?
Stephan Lee.
Stephan Lee who?
There's Stephan Lee something funny goin' on here.

Knock knock.
Who's there?
Jewel.
Jewel who?
Jewel love what I have for you.

Knock knock.
Who's there?
Joe King.
Joe King who?
I'm just Joe King with you! Hahaha...

Knock knock.
　　Who's there?
Evelyn.
　　Evelyn who?
If you're Evelyn town again, give me a call!

Knock knock.
　　Who's there?
Josie.
　　Josie who?
Did Josie the new movie that just came out?

Knock knock.
　　Who's there?
Marco.
　　Marco-?
Polo. Gotcha!

Knock knock.
　　Who's there?
Alby.
　　Alby who?
Alby waiting for you at the park.

Knock knock.
  Who's there?
Toad.
  Toad who?
I Toad you to open the door!

Knock knock.
  Who's there?
Nacho.
  Nacho who?
It's Nacho business who I am!

Knock knock.
  Who's there?
Mia.
  Mia who?
Are you gonna buy Mia new toy?

Knock knock.
  Who's there?
Quin.
  Quin who?
Quin are you gonna stop with these knock-knock jokes?

Knock knock.
  Who's there?
Eileen.
  Eileen who?
Can Eileen on you? I'm really tired.

Knock knock.
  Who's there?
Ren.
  Ren who?
Ren are you coming out to play?

Knock knock.
  Who's there?
Carrie.
  Carrie who?
Can you Carrie my backpack for me?

Knock knock.
  Who's there?
Nada.
  Nada who?
There's Nada single thing I want to do.

Knock knock.
　　Who's there?
Boris.
　　Boris who?
You Boris to death. Tell a better joke!

Knock knock.
　　Who's there?
Conrad.
　　Conrad who?
I'm here to Conrad-ulate you for a job well done.

Knock knock.
　　Who's there?
Jessie.
　　Jessie who?
Jessie for yourself!

Knock knock.
　　Who's there?
Troy.
　　Troy who?
Troy to understand what I'm saying to you, alright?

Knock knock.
>Who's there?

Aria.
>Aria who?

Aria coming out or not?

Knock knock.
>Who's there?

Chase.
>Chase who?

Chase me!

Knock knock.
>Who's there?

Monet.
>Monet who?

I've got no Monet left! Can you lend me some?

>**Fun Fact:** Did you know... Monet is a famous French painter who lived during the 18-1900s.

Knock knock.
>Who's there?

Camille.
>Camille who?

Would you like Camille after your work out?

Knock knock.
    Who's there?
Tamil.
    Tamil who?
Do you know how Tamil cows?

Knock knock.
    Who's there?
Phyllis.
    Phyllis who?
Can you Phyllis in on the news?

Knock knock.
    Who's there?
Lionel.
    Lionel who?
Lionel get you in trouble!

Knock knock.
    Who's there?
Toby.
    Toby who?
Toby or not Toby, that is the question.

Knock knock.
   Who's there?
Wyatt Lee.
   Wyatt Lee who?
Can you speak Wyatt Lee, please?

Knock knock.
   Who's there?
America.
   America who?
No, you heard wrong. I said I'm Erica.

Knock knock.
   Who's there?
Israel.
   Israel who?
Are you telling me that it Israel?

Knock knock.
   Who's there?
Canada.
   Canada who?
Can I have a Canada beans, please?

Knock knock.
    Who's there?
Moe.
        Moe who?
Can you give me some Moe money, please?

Knock knock.
    Who's there?
Jeremiah.
        Jeremiah who?
Do you know that Jeremiah best friend!

Knock knock.
    Who's there?
Shirley.
        Shirley who?
Shirley you remember my name!

Knock knock.
    Who's there?
Sonya.
        Sonya who?
What Sonya mind right now?

Knock knock.
Who's there?
Lacey.
Lacey who?
Stop being so Lacey and come out and play!

Knock knock.
Who's there?
Harold.
Harold who?
I Harold you got a new video game.

Knock knock.
Who's there?
Seymour.
Seymour who?
I want to Seymour movies with you.

Knock knock.
Who's there?
Utah.
Utah who?
I want Utah come out and play with me!

Knock knock.
Who's there?
Pizza delivery!
Took you long enough!

Ding dong.
Who's there?
The witch.
The witch who?
The witch is dead.

Knock knock.
Who's there?
Ryu.
Ryu who?
Ryu gonna open the door for me?

Knock knock.
Who's there?
Lena.
Lena who?
I need somebody to Lena on.

Knock knock.
Who's there?
Huda.
Huda who?
Huda thought that I'd still be here knocking on the door!

Knock knock.
Who's there?
Anwar.
Anwar who?
Anwar do you think you're going, young man?

Knock knock.
Who's there?
Ayla.
Ayla who?
Ayla wait for you out here, OK?

Knock knock.
Who's there?
Cindy.
Cindy who?
Are your parents Cindy apartment?

Knock knock.
Who's there?
Anita.
Anita who?
Anita hand, can you help?

Knock knock.
Who's there?
Thor.
Thor who?
Are you going to open the Thor or not?

> **Fun Fact:** Did you know... Thor is the God of Thunder in Norse mythology!

Knock knock.
Who's there?
Larry.
Larry who?
This joke is hi-Larry-ous!

Knock knock.
Who's there?
Nixon.
Nixon who?
You're Nixon line so get ready.

Knock knock.
> Who's there?

Joyce.
> Joyce who?

Do I have any Joyce but to wait for you out here?

Knock knock.
> Who's there?

Orange.
> Oh no you don't. I'm not falling for that one!

Knock knock.
> Who's there?

You said you were coming out!

Glossary Of Fun Facts

amoeba: a very small living thing found in water and soil.

Amsterdam: the capital city of the Netherlands, Europe.

android: a machine that looks and behaves like a human.

Andromeda: a galaxy about 2.2 million light years from the Milky Way.

baba ganoush: a dish from the Middle East made with eggplant mixed with onions, tomatoes, olive oil and other seasonings.

baklava: a pastry from the Middle East filled with nuts and honey.

barking up the wrong tree: not understanding or totally wrong.

bellhop: someone who works at a hotel and helps carry people's bags to their rooms.

blue cheese: a very strong type of cheese containing blue mold.

bookworm: someone who enjoys reading or studying.

borscht: a kind of Ukrainian soup with beets and other vegetables.

Buckingham Palace: a place in England where the royal family works and hosts events.

buzzkill: someone or something that stops people from enjoying themselves.

carpe diem: 'seize the day' in Latin. An expression meaning to enjoy the present and not worry about the future.

cat's got your tongue: you don't know what to say.

colibri: another word for hummingbird.

couch potato: somebody who is very lazy.

cyclops: a giant with one eye in the middle of its forehead.

dough: slang for 'money.'

escargot: 'snail' in French.

ewe: a female sheep.

fastest flight speed: the fastest flight speed is over 2000 mph.

FBI: the United States' intelligence and security service. It stands for 'Federal Bureau of Investigation.'

filling: a treatment you get for cavities at the dentist's.

flushed: red-faced and embarrassed.

full moon: it occurs once about every 27 days.

gingivitis: a kind of gum disease that makes your gums red and your breath smell.

googol: the number 1 followed by a hundred zeros.

Guten Tag: 'Hello' or 'Good day' in German.

hamstring: the soft part found behind your knees.

Hanukkah: a holiday celebrated by Jewish people.

hay fever: an allergy caused by dust or pollen.

iPhone: a smart phone made by Apple.

JASON: the first letters of the months between June and December.

je t'aime: 'I love you' in French.

kin: all the people in your family.

knock-knock jokes: a type of call and response joke, believed to be first used by Shakespeare.

laser tag: an activity people can do with laser guns.

lava: very hot, liquid rock.

litter: a group of puppies or kittens.

lychee: a white, juicy fruit from Asia.

Machu Picchu: a place in South America where the Inca lived.

Milky Way: the galaxy where our solar system and Earth is found.

Mona Lisa: a famous painting by Leonardo da Vinci.

Monet: a famous French painter.

Morse code: a way to send secret messages using clicking sounds or light.

nectar: a sweet, sugary liquid that plants produce to attract insects such as bees.

Neymar: a Brazilian soccer player.

orca: another name for killer whale.

phytoplankton: very small living things found in oceans and fresh water bodies.

Pig Latin: a made-up language used by kids to speak in code.

purple popcorn: popcorn with purple food coloring.

roadrunner: a small, brown and white bird that lives in the desert and can run very fast.

Saint Bernard: the biggest breed of dog in the world.

supercalifragilisticexpialidocious: a word that doesn't actually mean anything. Used to say that something is very good.

shellfish: a type of aquatic animal that has a shell, such as oysters, lobsters, and crabs.

sidekick: a close friend or companion who follows you everywhere on adventures.

Sign Language: a way to talk to other people by using your hands.

sphinx: a giant statue by the pyramids of Egypt.

Starbucks: an American coffee shop with over 20,000 locations around the world.

taboo: something unacceptable or not allowed.

take a rain check: change an appointment to another day.

Thanksgiving: a holiday celebrated in North America. Canadians celebrate it in October, while Americans celebrate it in November.

to not click with someone: to not get along with someone.

to not give a hoot: to not care about something.

Thor: the Norse god of thunder.

Timbuktu: a city in Mali, Africa.

Transylvania: a region in Romania, Europe.

U2: an Irish rock band.

utopia: a place where everything is perfect.

Web: another word for the Internet.

wisdom teeth: teeth that you starting growing at around 20 years old.

Wurst: 'sausage' in German.

your goose is cooked: you're in big trouble!

zamboni: a vehicle used to clean and smooth the surface of ice.

Zuckerberg: 'sugar mountain' in German.

About The Author

J.J. Wiggins worked in the IT industry where he enjoyed a long and fruitful, yet tedious career. He has since retired and now spends his days with his family, doing his darndest to make them laugh.

http://amazon.com/author/jjwiggins

Thanks for reading!

Did you have a good laugh?

62549945R00059

Made in the USA
Lexington, KY
10 April 2017